D0869257

Ben Hur

Lew Wallace

Academic Industries, Inc.
West Haven, Connecticut 06516

ISBN 0-88301-736-9

Published by
Academic Industries, Inc.
The Academic Building
Saw Mill Road
West Haven, Connecticut 06516

Printed in the United States of America

about the author

Lew Wallace was born in 1827 in Brookville, Indiana. Fighting with the Union army during the Civil War, he was promoted to the rank of major general. As a practicing lawyer and politician, he served as governor of the New Mexico Territory and as the U.S. minister to Turkey.

Wallace's most famous novel, *Ben Hur*, helped make the historical novel popular as a literary form. In the story, Judah Ben-Hur, a Jewish nobleman, is unjustly imprisoned. When he escapes, his path somehow crosses the path of Christ. Later, after the crucifixion, Ben-Hur devotes his great fortune to further Christianity.

Two other novels, *The Fair God* and *The Prince of India*, helped make Wallace one of the most widely-read authors of the nineteenth century. After a distinguished career as a diplomat and writer, he died in Crawfordsville, Indiana, in 1905.

Lew Wallace

Ben Hur

Judah Ben-Hur

Messala

Esther

Simonides

At one time, the soldiers of Rome had beaten the armies of all other countries. Rome ruled all the known world. But many people dreamed of the day when they would be free again. In Judea, the priests of the Jewish people told of a King who would come to save them.

He will be born in Bethelehem . . . to be King of the Jews . . . and He shall rule all the earth!

One December day, Balthasar, an Egyptian, traveled for many hours in the Arabian desert.

At noon he looked around him, nodded, pulled the camel to a stop, and stepped upon the sand.

At last, this is the place!

Taking food from the camel's pack, he set up a tent and spread out a feast.

They will come. He that led me will lead them!

Soon two more camels drew near from different directions.

Peace be with you!

And with you. See, the other comes!

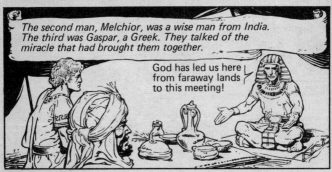

The second man, Melchior, was a wise man from India. The third was Gaspar, a Greek. They talked of the miracle that had brought them together.

God has led us here from faraway lands to this meeting!

He will lead us on, to find the baby born to be King of the Jews!

We will kneel and worship Him— so that men may learn that heaven is won not by the sword, but by faith and love.

Later the three wise men started out on their journey. Suddenly, in the darkness, they saw a bright light.

The star! The star! God is with us!

Following the star, they came to a stable in Bethlehem in which some poor travelers were spending the night.

Is there not a new-born child here?

Yes, a babe was born last night.

Show Him to us! We have come to worship Him!

Inside, they found Joseph, Mary, and the baby. They knelt down and worshipped Him.

It is He, the Savior!

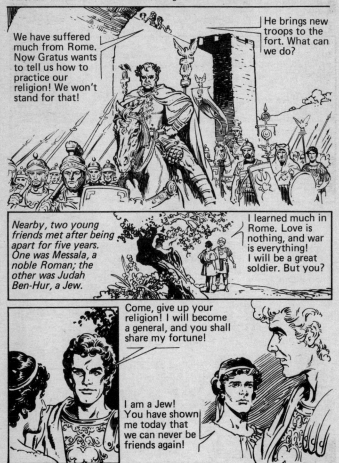

Later, the wise men went on their way. The baby grew up as the Romans continued to rule Judea. Twenty years passed. Then Valerius Gratus was named the new governor of Judea.

We have suffered much from Rome. Now Gratus wants to tell us how to practice our religion! We won't stand for that!

He brings new troops to the fort. What can we do?

Nearby, two young friends met after being apart for five years. One was Messala, a noble Roman; the other was Judah Ben-Hur, a Jew.

I learned much in Rome. Love is nothing, and war is everything! I will be a great soldier. But you?

Come, give up your religion! I will become a general, and you shall share my fortune!

I am a Jew! You have shown me today that we can never be friends again!

11

Here we part! The peace of God be with you.

So be it, then! Down Eros, up Mars!

Sadly, Judah Ben-Hur returned home. There he was met by Amrah, his old nurse.

Your mother asks for you. She is on the roof.

I will go to her.

In the summerhouse on the roof, he greeted his mother.

Something is worrying you, my son!

Yes. I have been to see Messala.

I have heard Messala mock others. But today he made fun of me and my God! I parted with him forever.

Mother, are we truly lower than the Romans? Why may not a son of Israel do anything a Roman may do?

Messala comes from a noble family. But both your family and your race are far older and more noble than his!

As for what you may do—so long as you serve the Lord God of Israel and not Rome, you may do anything!

I may be a soldier?

So long as you serve the Lord, you have my permission!

Happy again, Judah fell asleep. When he awoke the next morning, his young sister, Tirzah, sat by his side, singing.

A very pretty song, Tirzah!

I was told to wake you. Your breakfast is ready.

Amrah brought breakfast, and they talked as they ate.

What do you think? I am going to Rome to learn to be a soldier!

But you would not fight for *Rome?*

War is a trade. To learn it, one must go to school—and there is no school like a Roman camp.

I will fight for Rome, and in return she will teach me how to fight against her some day!

Suddenly the sound of army trumpets rang out. They rushed to the roof.

Roman soldiers from the fort!

Then came an officer riding alone.

Look! It is Gratus, the new Roman commander!

As Judah leaned forward to look, a broken tile fell from under his hand.

The tile struck Gratus on the head. He fell.

Oh, Tirzah!

From below there were shouts and cries as soldiers broke into the courtyard.

Don't be afraid! I will explain that it was an accident.

Mother! Mother!

There is the one who tried to kill Gratus! And his mother and sister. You have the whole family!

They have done nothing, Messala! Remember our friendship and help them, I pray you!

But Messala turned away.

I cannot help you. I must leave.

I pray you, Lord, that someday my hand may punish him for the way he has acted in this hour!

Judah Ben-Hur was judged guilty and marched away.

17

After starting out, Quintus went to the great cabin to study his men.

Perhaps I can replace the weakest of these men with stronger prisoners from the pirate ships.

The slaves were known only by numbers, according to their places on the ship.

Number sixty is easy and graceful. He looks good!

Number sixty was Judah Ben-Hur. He turned, and Quintus saw his face.

A Jew! And only a boy! I must know more of him.

Judah moved his oar more slowly as he met Quintus's kindly look—and the whip of the rower chief cracked down.

Mind your oar! Don't slow your pace!

Later, Quintus spoke to the chief.

What do you know of the youth at number sixty?

Only that he is my best rower. He always does as he is told.

If I am on deck when he is resting, send him to me.

Yes, noble Quintus!

Several hours later, as Quintus Arrius watched the sea, Judah drew near. Quintus questioned him.

The chief tells me you are his best rower. You are very young. And from your speech, you are a Jew.

And proud that I am a Jew!

I knew one prince of Jerusalem, Ithamar, of the House of Hur. He sailed the seas as a merchant. He was fit to have been a king!

I am only a slave now, but he was my father.

A son of Hur—you! What brought you here?

They said I tried to kill Gratus, the Roman commander.

You? All Rome rang with the story! But I thought the family of Hur was wiped from the earth afterward.

My mother—and my little sister, Tirzah! For three long years I have heard not a word. Oh, noble sir, tell me what you know.

Were you guilty?

By the God of my fathers—I swear I am innocent!

Judah told of the accident with the tile; of how he was dragged away without a real trial and made a galley slave. Quintus was shocked. A fair man, he believed Judah.

It was near dawn when they sighted the pirate fleet that had been robbing Roman towns.

The pirate ships are near.

Good!

Quintus ordered the sailors to the deck.

Up and ready!

Extra arrows and javelins were stacked on deck. Oil tanks and fire-balls were made ready.

Below deck, the slaves knew a battle was coming. They were chained to their benches at such a time.

Chained, there was no chance of escape if the ship were sunk. Would Quintus Arrius say that Judah need not be chained?

Judah had hope. But the chief reached him at last. He held out his foot.

Then Quintus nodded and the chief went to him.

How strong he is!

And what spirit he has! He does better without the chains. Leave them off!

Grateful, Judah bent to his oar. The ship moved on. Suddenly there was a great crash as their ship was rammed by another.

The men below could hear trumpets blowing, and the sounds of men fighting on deck. Smoke poured into the galley.

The slaves struggled to tear loose from their chains. Judah leaped for the stairs.

Quintus Arrius is my one chance to be free! What if he should be killed? I must find him and protect him.

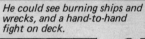

He could see burning ships and wrecks, and a hand-to-hand fight on deck.

Suddenly the floor seemed to lift and break to pieces. He fell backward.

The sea rushed in.

He sank down and down under the sea. Something pushed against him and he grabbed it.

Then he rose again, reached the surface, and gasped for air.

The battle still raged around him. Ships were burning. Men tossed overboard still fought each other.

Suddenly, beside him, a drowning man appeared.

Quintus! Quintus!

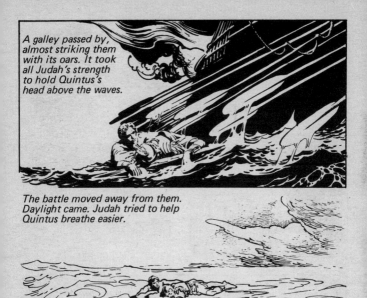

A galley passed by, almost striking them with its oars. It took all Judah's strength to hold Quintus's head above the waves.

The battle moved away from them. Daylight came. Judah tried to help Quintus breathe easier.

I see what you have done. You have saved my life at the risk of your own!

If we live through this, I will do everything I can to show my thanks!

Suddenly Judah pointed to the north.

Look! A ship coming this way!

Of what land? Can you see a flag?

I cannot tell. There is no flag.

A Roman ship would have flags out. It must be a pirate ship.

The pirates will spare your life. But I shall drown with my ship rather than face capture!

Wait! There is a helmet on top of the mast. And a small boat is picking up men who are floating nearby.

By the helmet and the rescue, I know a Roman ship! We are saved!

I knew your father and loved him! I will make you my son. And we will follow the pirate ships and sink them all!

Quintus was welcomed on the galley as a hero. His ships closed in on the remaining pirates and crushed them. Many pirate ships were captured.

Arriving on land again, Quintus told of his rescue. Then he presented Judah.

My friends, this is my son who shall be known by my name. I pray you to love him as you love me.

Quintus Arrius was honored for the victory and was rewarded by the emperor with gifts that made him very rich. Later he adopted Judah by law. For some time Judah lived with him as his son at a villa in Rome.

If you wish to be a wise man, my son, I will hire the most famous teacher in Rome for you.

My greatest wish is to learn the art of war!

So it was. In the gymnasium, Judah learned the skills of the gladiators.

In the camps, he learned to use weapons.

He learned to ride horses, and to take part in chariot races.

Five years passed, and Judah became a man. Quintus died at sea, and Judah grew very rich. Now he wanted to lead men in battle, so he sailed from Rome to Antioch to join in a war against the Parthians. One day, he overheard two men talking.

Many of these ships fly bright yellow flags. Do you know what they mean?

They belong to a rich trader named Simonides.

Perhaps you have heard of a prince of Jerusalem named Hur. He was a merchant many years ago.

Simonides was in charge of Hur's business in Antioch. Hur was lost at sea, but the business did well.

31

Then the prince's young son tried to kill the Roman commander, Gratus. The boy has not been heard of since. No one of the family was left alive.

Their palace was closed. Gratus took all of the Hur riches he could find.

And Simonides?

He opened trade on his own— sent out caravans —and now has galleys enough to make a royal fleet of ships! But he paid dearly.

How was that?

Twice Gratus has had him beaten, trying to make him admit that his wealth belonged to the Hurs so that Gratus could take it. Now Simonides is old and crippled.

Judah's ship docked at Antioch. On shore, because of the story he had overheard, Judah changed his plans. He would visit Simonides.

The rich merchant lived at his place of business.

Now at last I may hear news of home—and mother—and dear little Tirzah!

Judah entered and looked around.

If Simonides is really my father's slave, he will not want to give up this rich business to me!

A man approached Judah.

I want to see Simonides, the merchant.

Will you come this way?

Judah followed him through the warehouse and up a staircase. They came out on a rooftop bright with flowers. A small house was was built in the middle.

A stranger to see the master!

Let him enter.

Entering the room, Judah found himself facing a crippled old man and a lovely young girl. He bowed.

I am Judah, son of the House of Hur. I have heard that you knew my father!

I knew the Prince Hur. We did business together. Sit, I pray you!

My loves are few. One is this dear soul, my daughter Esther.

My other love was for a whole family—if only I knew where they were!

My mother and sister! You speak of them?

Before I speak of the Hur family, you must show me proof of who you are.

Proof? But—I have no proof that I am my father's son. Those who could tell you are lost—or dead!

For the first time he saw that his years as a galley slave had wiped out all proof that he was a Hur. The Romans knew him well, but only as a son of Arrius.

Good Simonides, I can only tell my story.

I will listen.

Judah told of the accident, his arrest, and his years on the galley. He told of saving Quintus, of being adopted, and of inheriting much money when Quintus died.

So you see, I want no money. I want only news of my mother and my sister! I beg you to tell me of them!

After the accident with the roof tile, I have nothing to tell you. They are lost.

Then another hope is broken! I have nothing now to live for but revenge! I thank you both. Farewell.

May peace go with you.

Hardly had Judah left than Simonides turned to Esther.

Quick! Ring for Malluch!

The young man just leaving, Malluch—follow him, make friends with him. Learn all about his habits and his life. Then report what you learn to me. Hurry!

I shall do as you say, master!

As Judah walked through the city, Malluch followed. Soon he was able to talk to Judah.

Chariot races are starting at the stadium there. Would you care to see them?

Yes, indeed! I have some skill in racing, too.

36

They found seats and watched the chariots. As the last one passed the stand, the driver lost control of his horses.

That Roman! He said he could drive them! I was a fool to trust a Roman!

As the horses were quieted, Judah turned to Malluch.

They are the finest animals I have ever seen! I can understand the owner's worry. Who is he?

A great and rich man from the desert— Sheik Ilderim.

As Judah and Malluch left the stands, a man began to speak to the crowd.

Hear me, men! The good Sheik Ilderim, with four beautiful horses, needs a mighty man to drive them in the great race! Whoever can do this, he will make rich!

Thinking hard, Judah followed Malluch out. As they drew near the Fountain of Castalia, they saw other visitors.

A prince from far away!

More likely a king—and a beautiful girl.

The camel got down on its knees. The driver began to fill a cup with water. Suddenly there came the sound of a chariot and horses. In great fear, the people rushed away.

Look out! The Roman will ride us down!

Stop! Back!

There was but one chance. Judah caught the reins of the nearest horses.

You Roman! Do you care so little for human life?

When the horses were quiet, Messala walked over to the girl.

Please forgive me. I am Messala. I did not see you or the camel.

But she would not speak to him. She turned to Judah.

Will you fill the cup? My father would like some water.

I am your most willing servant!

As Messala moved away, the girl looked after him.

You are beautiful! And you will see me again!

The camel rose, and the old man called Judah to him.

In the holy name of the one God, I thank you. I am Balthasar, the Egyptian. We are the guests of Sheik Ilderim. Please visit us in his tents.

Thank you. I will.

39

I know the Roman! He stood by and laughed when my family was taken away. He knows the secret I would give my life for—whether my mother and sister are still alive!

He must live until I learn that secret. But I can punish him if you will help me!

He is a Roman and I am a Jew! I will help you!

In a few words, Judah told his story to Malluch.

He asked Malluch about the great games soon to be held, in which Messala would race.

Malluch agreed to take him to Sheik Ilderim.

The sheik's camp was an hour away. They talked as they rode.

Sheik Ilderim hates the Romans! He looks forward to the coming of the King of the Jews as the prophets tell.

Malluch knew Sheik Ilderim through Simonides. At the camp they were welcomed. Later Malluch took Judah aside.

I have told the sheik about you. He will let you try the horses tomorrow.

So be it!

The sheik welcomed Judah and led him into his tent.

Supper is here—and my friend Balthasar also. He has a story to tell which an Israelite should never tire of hearing.

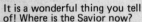

Once again Judah met the old man of the fountain, Balthasar.

Today my life was in danger. It would have been lost had not this youth stepped in and saved me!

After supper, Judah heard from Balthasar about the meeting of the three wise men twenty-seven years before. He heard how they followed the star to Bethlehem to worship the King of the Jews.

It is a wonderful thing you tell of! Where is the Savior now?

I think He is in Judea, and will soon make Himself known. But His kingdom will be not of earth, but of heaven.

You talk in riddles. I do not understand.

Nor do I! Every leader must have earthly power!

But there is a kingdom greater than the earth.

In the morning, the sheik took Judah to his horses.

I will have them harnessed and a chariot brought.

For today I will ride the fifth horse, bareback. And I will harness them myself.

Judah sprang to the horse's back.

I must learn to know each horse and what he can do. And each must know me.

Later Judah drove the horses in straight lines and in circles. He walked them, trotted, galloped.

I am well pleased! He has done more in two hours than the Roman driver could do in a month!

Malluch returned, and Judah asked for his help.

Find out where our chariot will stand in the starting gate. Try to learn if Messala's chariot is light or heavy. More important, find out how high his axle is above the ground!

It shall be done!

He warned the sheik.

The Romans have many tricks. Let no stranger see the horses. Have them watched night and day.

No strange hand shall come near them!

Now, since you know Latin, read for me these reports I have just received.

Of course!

Judah thought that Messala had not known him. But he was wrong. Upon seeing his old enemy still alive, Messala had written a message to Gratus. A copy had come into the sheik's hands, but he could not read it.

Judah began to read. Suddenly his face turned white and his hands shook.

It is from Messala to Gratus!

Well, I am waiting . . .

He reminds Gratus that the two of them planned that all the Hur family would die. They wanted to divide our riches between themselves.

But he asks Gratus if my mother and sister are still alive! He does not *know* if they are dead! There is still hope!

He says that I must be killed. And that "the traitor, Sheik Ilderim, will soon be sent to Rome as a slave!"

I—a freeman—to Rome! My free people, slaves! You shall have men, horses, camels, everything I own, to use against Rome!

Later that day, Judah and Ilderim visited Simonides. He agreed that Judah was really of the Hur family.

Then he gave Judah the fortune he had made in business for them. But Judah would take only a small part of it.

Then they talked of Balthasar's story. They spoke, too, of what should be done with the fortune.

I was already rich with the money of Quintus Arrius. Now comes this greater fortune!

The baby the wise men saw— the King, when He comes—He will be poor.

When the King appears, I will give every cent to help Him!

Go and find the men, Judah. Choose captains, and train them in secret. Hide the weapons that I will send you.

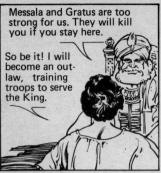

Messala and Gratus are too strong for us. They will kill you if you stay here.

So be it! I will become an outlaw, training troops to serve the King.

But not until after the race! I don't think I will be in danger from Gratus that soon.

Many people were betting on the race. The next day Judah spoke to Malluch.

Can you get Messala to bet a large sum of money on himself against me? Why should I not win back what he has stolen from me?

No Roman could think that he would be beaten by a Jew. Soon Malluch brought word that Messala had bet his whole fortune on the race.

About Messala's chariot. Its axle stands a good hand higher from the ground than yours does.

So much higher? Good!

In the parade the day of the race, the chariot drivers were cheered by the great crowd.

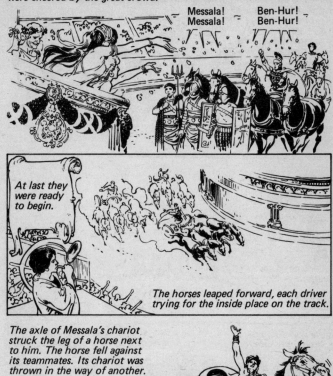

Messala! Messala!

Ben-Hur! Ben-Hur!

At last they were ready to begin.

The horses leaped forward, each driver trying for the inside place on the track.

The axle of Messala's chariot struck the leg of a horse next to him. The horse fell against its teammates. Its chariot was thrown in the way of another.

Several men carried off the unlucky driver and led the horses away. The race went on. Messala and Ben-Hur rode side by side ahead of everyone.

They were coming to a turn, the hardest part of the race. Suddenly Messala shouted. His whip lashed out, striking the sheik's horses who had never before been touched except with love.

Out of my way!

The crowd roared with anger. But Ben-Hur's hands, strong from three years at the oars, held the frightened horses.

Astair, Rigel, Antares—good horses! Steady boys—it's all right. . . .

He kept control of his team, and the turn was made. The two chariots raced on as the crowd cheered.

Do you see Messala? He is as handsome as Apollo!

Is he so much more handsome than Ben-Hur?

Side by side they came to the last turn. Suddenly Ben-Hur moved his team to the left. The wheel of his chariot caught Messala's wheel.

There was a crash. The axle of the Roman's chariot struck the earth.

People stood on their seats and cheered as Judah and his horses flew down the track to the finish line.

Ben-Hur was crowned the winner of the great race.

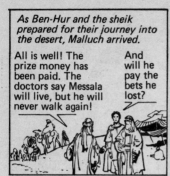

As Ben-Hur and the sheik prepared for their journey into the desert, Malluch arrived.

All is well! The prize money has been paid. The doctors say Messala will live, but he will never walk again!

And will he pay the bets he lost?

If he pays, he is ruined! If he does not pay, he will lose his family's good name!

In any case, the glory is ours!

Once again, Judah began a new life, this time in the desert. Simonides, by paying a large sum of money to the Roman emperor, had Gratus removed as ruler of Judea. This made it safer for Ben-Hur to search for his loved ones.

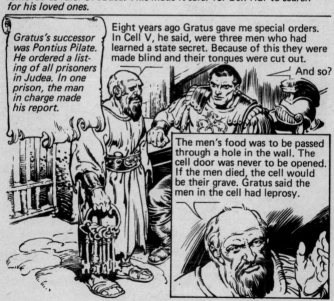

Gratus's successor was Pontius Pilate. He ordered a listing of all prisoners in Judea. In one prison, the man in charge made his report.

Eight years ago Gratus gave me special orders. In Cell V, he said, were three men who had learned a state secret. Because of this they were made blind and their tongues were cut out.

And so?

The men's food was to be passed through a hole in the wall. The cell door was never to be opened. If the men died, the cell would be their grave. Gratus said the men in the cell had leprosy.

49

Today in listing the prisoners, I went to Cell V. I found only one old man.

And for all these years food had been sent for three?

I had the old man washed and cared for, and told him to go free. Instead, by signs he told me to go back with him to the cell!

In the cell he led me to a hole in the back wall.

Hello! Is someone there?

A woman of Israel and her daughter. Help us quickly, or we will die!

That is very strange. Let us rescue the women!

The door has been walled up. I have sent for workmen with tools.

For eight years Tirzah and her mother had lived in a prison. The only light came through the same small hole through which they received their food. Now they heard the tools of workmen. A pile of stones fell. They saw light!

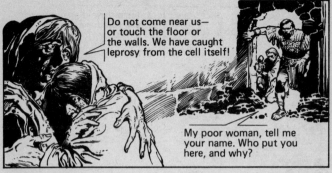

Do not come near us— or touch the floor or the walls. We have caught leprosy from the cell itself!

My poor woman, tell me your name. Who put you here, and why?

I am the widow of Prince Ben-Hur. Gratus put us here. Why I do not know, unless he wanted our fortune.

I will send you food and drink.

And clothes, and water for bathing, we pray you!

That shall be done. Make ready, and tonight you will be taken to the gate and set free.

Lepers were not allowed to live with other people or even come near them. They had to beg for food. They lived in a graveyard on a hill outside the city. They had to warn anyone who came near them by crying "unclean!"

So that night they were out of prison under the stars, free at last—but free for what?

Let us go for a last look at our old home. When morning comes, they will put us out of the city gate—to return no more.

Yes, lepers have no homes. We belong to the dead!

51

That same night, a traveler reached the city. It was Judah, coming to search for his loved ones where he last saw them. Simonides had told him that Amrah, their servant, still lived like a ghost in the Hur palace.

THIS IS THE PROPERTY OF THE EMPEROR

But his knocking brought no answer. He sat on the doorstep to wait, and fell asleep.

God is good! It is my son, your brother! Let us look at him once more.

Judah! My brother!

Do not go near him! We are lepers. Do you want him to become a leper also?

So they proved their love and watched from the shadows as Amrah came to the gate.

Oh, Amrah, it is you! Speak! Tell me of Mother and Tirzah!

I weep with joy to see you. But I know nothing of them!

Judah spent the night in his old home. Early in the morning, Amrah went to buy food. By chance she stood next to a workman who had broken into the prison cell the day before.

"I am the widow of Prince Ben-Hur," she said, "put here by Gratus!" There they were, in prison for eight years, and their bodies eaten up by leprosy!

They speak of Judah's mother.

Weeping for joy, Amrah hurried home. She could tell Judah she had found his mother! But then what? He would rush to her and would catch the disease.

She went to the well where the lepers got their daily water. Two women drew near—but they were old! At first she could not believe it was they.

Oh, my mistress, thank God I have found you!

You must not tell Judah where we are or that you have seen us!

He shall not become what we are! You will bring us food each day—and tell us of Judah—but to him you will say nothing.

It will be hard, my mistress, but I will do as you say.

So Amrah kept the secret. And Judah went into Galilee, where he found many young men ready to fight for the coming King against Rome. In secret, in the countryside, he trained them.

Before the winter was over, he had raised three legions and taught them the use of arms.

Let the good King come! We can win a war for Him!

In camp one night a horseman arrived bringing a letter.

The waiting is ended! A prophet says the King is coming. He will be at the River Jordan.

Go home. Send word to those under you to be ready.

By midnight he was riding south through the desert. Late the next day, stopping to camp, he met Balthasar and his daughter, Iras.

I remember you said He would be a king, but that His kingdom is of heaven, not of this world.

I still believe so. You expect to meet a King of men.

Later he walked with beautiful Iras.

This King will be the most powerful in the world! And I will earn His richest gifts—perhaps even a kingdom myself!

And I shall be your queen. And we will be happy forever!

The next morning they reached the river where a crowd was waiting. They saw John, the prophet, and a stranger.

Look! This is the Son of God!

It is He, the Son of God, whom I have seen again!

If He is really a king, He will show it.

Nearly three years passed. Every day the King became more of a mystery to Ben-Hur. But he kept on training soldiers to serve Him. In late March he returned to his own house, where Balthasar and Iras now lived.

Simonides and Esther were there. Judah told them of the King.

What would you say of a man who could be rich? He could make gold from the stones at His feet, yet He is poor because He wants to be!

You saw it?

Yes. And the sick have only to touch His robe to be cured!

55

"You are clean," He said to a leper, and the man grew healthy! Ten lepers came to Him together one day and He cured them all! I was there and saw it!

Such a thing was never heard of before!

As usual the next morning, Amrah went to find her mistress. But instead of waiting near the well, she climbed to the graveyard.

What have you done! Now you can no longer return home! You will be a leper like us!

I have come to take you to a wonderful man who has power to cure you! It is true—I heard it from Judah!

It must be the Messiah!

He will walk today on the road to Jerusalem! We must hurry to find Him!

They climbed a steep hill. Though weak and ill, they walked on.
Reaching the road, they saw a crowd.

Blessed is the King of Israel who comes in the name of the Lord.

We must get nearer, my child! He cannot hear us!

She moved forward and called out to Him.

Oh, Master, You are the Messiah! You can make us clean. Have mercy!

Woman, your faith is great! May it be as you wish!

The crowd moved on. The sounds died away.

Daughter, I have his promise! We are saved!

As usual that day, Judah was following Christ. He heard the prayer of the woman and waited to see what would happen to her.

My mother! And Tirzah! Tell me if I am really seeing you!

Oh, master! How good our God is!

They were cured! They ran to him with open arms.

Mother! Tirzah!

Oh, my children! Let us give thanks to the Messiah who has His power from God!

Before they could enter the city, the mother and daughter had to be checked by a doctor. Meanwhile, Judah had tents set up for them.

You are armed, my son. Is it a time of war?

No, but I may have to fight for the Messiah.

Who are his enemies?

The Romans who do not want Him to be a king. Some of our rabbis, too, are against Him. They do not like the way He welcomes those who are not Jews!

Soon after, the Messiah was arrested and sentenced to die on the cross. But even though they begged Him, He would not allow Judah and his men to fight for Him.

Sadly Judah went back to his house. There he found Iras looking like a person he had never seen before.

Tell me—where now is the Son of God from whom we wanted so much? Has He fought against Rome?

Where is His palace? Where is His kingdom—the one I was to share with you?

The King! The Son of God! The Redeemer of the world! Ha, ha, ha!

You are kinder than you think. You quickly teach me not to love you. Let us go our own ways and forget we ever met.

Leaving, he stopped at the summerhouse thinking he would see Simonides. Instead, there was Esther, asleep.

Here is one I could truly love . . . beautiful and kind. I will not wake her now. But later . . .

A great crowd of people came to watch the crucifixion. Many were there to make fun of the dying man, others to weep and pray.

Several years later, Judah, his wife Esther, and their children were sitting with Simonides. Suddenly news came that a new emperor, Nero, was killing the Christians in Rome.

I knew long ago that my great fortune was to be used for the Lord. But how can I best help now?

Go to Rome. The Romans hold burial places sacred. You can build places for prayer underground. If you build them near the graveyards, the Romans will not come near.

It is a great idea! I will sail for Rome tomorrow. And you, Esther?

My husband, I will go with you and help you to serve Christ!

If one visits, today, the ancient catacomb of San Calixto, he will see what became of the fortune of Ben-Hur. In those great underground rooms the Christians prayed, and one day they came forth free to spread Christ's teaching.

THE END

COMPLETE LIST OF POCKET CLASSICS AVAILABLE

CLASSICS

C 1 Black Beauty
C 2 The Call of the Wild
C 3 Dr. Jekyll and Mr. Hyde
C 4 Dracula
C 5 Frankenstein
C 6 Huckleberry Finn
C 7 Moby Dick
C 8 The Red Badge of Courage
C 9 The Time Machine
C10 Tom Sawyer
C11 Treasure Island
C12 20,000 Leagues Under the Sea
C13 The Great Adventures of Sherlock Holmes
C14 Gulliver's Travels
C15 The Hunchback of Notre Dame
C16 The Invisible Man
C17 Journey to the Center of the Earth
C18 Kidnapped
C19 The Mysterious Island
C20 The Scarlet Letter
C21 The Story of My Life
C22 A Tale of Two Cities
C23 The Three Musketeers
C24 The War of the Worlds
C25 Around the World in Eighty Days
C26 Captains Courageous
C27 A Connecticut Yankee in King Arthur's Court
C28 The Hound of the Baskervilles
C29 The House of the Seven Gables
C30 Jane Eyre
C31 The Last of the Mohicans
C32 The Best of O. Henry
C33 The Best of Poe
C34 Two Years Before the Mast
C35 White Fang
C36 Wuthering Heights
C37 Ben Hur
C38 A Christmas Carol
C39 The Food of the Gods
C40 Ivanhoe
C41 The Man in the Iron Mask
C42 The Prince and the Pauper
C43 The Prisoner of Zenda
C44 The Return of the Native
C45 Robinson Crusoe
C46 The Scarlet Pimpernel

COMPLETE LIST OF POCKET CLASSICS AVAILABLE
(cont'd)